T0303561

SOUND REMAINS

John Tritica

SOUND REMAINS

CHAX PRESS   TUCSON

I wish to express thanks to the editors of the following journals
where some of these poems first appeared:
*Café Review, First Intensity, Harwood Review, Hotel Amerika,
House Organ, o•blēk, Situation, Talisman.*

ISBN: 978-0-925904-59-1

Cover painting: *What the Bee Knows* — JB Bryan
oil on canvas

Set in Dante with titling in Kerning
Book Design: JB Bryan

Chax Press
650 East Ninth St.
Tucson, AZ 85705-8584

contents

LIFT OFF Leaning

for Mary Rising Higgins

1

A bite of peach tart, a double espresso.

My books pile up the table.

Ice-minded, the lemon floats on top.

The far night plumed, exits exhumed.

In the exhibit we call exhilaration
sight inside scoops the room.

Shattered narration, the electronic world hiccups.

Serious stars, a high pressure night.

The hug's representation's a flame
whose phosphorous bestows.

Another sip of espresso lingers on the palate.

She walks across Central
purple dress, ink in wind.

A slight disturbance in frequency
receptions away.

Savor the taste, tongue alive on teeth.

2

After carving out the time
they awaken too early.

Buzz side night born feeling,
propensity optimal, site and seedling.

A walk is not just a walk
chill shadows reel about the ground.

Skip up step tempo
signing in light wind.

A matter of hearing what's slight significant.

Leave it in sound time
practice as the spring is in sight.

The stillness is illusory
broom grass sifts the breeze.

Glass table top cold, 7:09 am.

I surround myself
with the movement of *oclock*.

Threaten the ecstatic, frighten the mundane.

To practice flame . . .

At any point an energy contact
as space scissors what's temporal.

The book can fire on any page.

Significance of the struggle
in a varied code, urgent innovation.

When continuity's uncertain,
all's base metal.

Out of the jaws of *expanding vacancy*
the plenum's light release.

From cellular aberration to days' relief.

Gale force tenacity, verbal asanas,
collide, pushing comfort, destiny cease.

Walking toward the other, the pause in please.

3

I reconnoiter among Russian sage.

A web of droplets shines in suspension.

A necklace of geese overcomes the sky.

Present tense in spine and skin.

Whip flight marginal,
winged dialogue, traces find trees.

High pressure sky echoes aqua
azure wide, white shirt flaps on the line.

Is of the world through sparking.

Seed live espresso, what I hear's
enhanced in its leading.

Sit in the exact location
of shape, sown leaves.

Is said what sorts words out:
compliance, coincidence, placement, stream.

Full moon, spotted wind, first day
of spring.

Reinhabit the body of found survival
an echo from the mesa sounds.

Like a series of floors that lift off leaning.

A structure always just out of reach
but in stretching we believe.

Not just a story, finding in shadows
where *everything you respond to* leaves you complete.

quotes: Mary Rising Higgins, oclock

LIGHT as LOCaTIon

for Jeff Bryan

I catch sight of it
under the pier where
slots of light float on wave
foam and eye brushes
ocean water to mirror
back a rhythm, a density in
key signature, a part or
together where location
happens as a tension
in the music. Not
the sublime, but bits

of dried grapeleaves windshift
remains from the hailstorm.
A cat out the corner
of the eye. Those slots
stretch light like
singing through a saxophone.

In sign own expression
I leave the blinds drawn
in this heat. Not to hide
or distort, but to write
just above the outstretched hand.

I include voice side kneeling
a feel for size and weight.
Tensile strength night born breathing
where each word counts its seat.
Sound out a quiet underneath.
Side voice revealing
alphabet, number, angle, time.
A plate shatters, attention
turns naked, returns refreshed.
In the interstices under the pier
a view clears about the planked shade.

on ocean to see

Cormorant stretched over kayak's tip.

Waves gnash rocks on shore.

Gull picks balance search
for castoffs.

Wave boards hit sand line speeding.

Phase of moon tide travels.

A jet invisible in the sky now
side up wing, gone sightless again.

Find distinct sound in
each wave, hold it inside

Drift subsides in a round.

Break and re-break, play
on wave mist, to disperse on water mirror.

Sky reflects a house of signs.

Whiteness on green
caves underneath.

Only if dolphins swim with
pelican dives in a knot of kelp

Bubbles in diet that feeds.

Place it beside the bougainvillea
towers, a hummingbird flees.

Each facet of light on wet sand.

Moment's rest over breakers
paddles on.

In the midst of crowds
follows in and out ocean, breath.

Not alone but in motion tide
rhythm ear follows flow.

Sea kayak like turning a truck.

Neck extension
eucalyptus, orange in blossom

Up the hill, traffic
in tidal sound echoes.

Grilled vegetables, pasta salad,
a sip of ale on the beach.

Waves wash parting, power
to seize, not limit rapidity or speed.

In a round wide teeming
energy of ocean air leads.

Moment's Aroma

for Tom Guralnick

A swing into sound makes
play available. A tenderness
recovers its way. In space
notion its demeanor woven.

If I could disappear in
a thousand departures
still here. Bicycle,
mirror, pond, train.

With lens expose motion.
How ink sky blues you.
In rivulets, torrents, nights
retrieve a moment's aroma.

Not news items, energy
that skates the neurons,
strikes a blaze, remakes
the obvious oblique.

Sit in sorts of song.
Salute what flavors the tongue:
blueberry, pomegranate, pinot noir.

The first note ready
sharp enough to quicken.

In mix alto tone bends his
sound into shapes that tender.
I assume that the room circulates

piano cascade surrounds.
In some rare mode
known in another key
blooms rehearsed invisibly.

As extension of The Space, now
breathless as final touch
never further than fiction.

Frank Morgan and John Hicks
at the Outpost Performance Space
10.IV.00, Albuquerque, NM

sound remains

Erik Satie's "Nocturnes," performed by France Clidat

Still on the active edge.

Not clamor, the sure step
to organize a frayed perception.

The boy pulls the blinds
ribbons reflect the page

As if to start cicadas.

A swarm of cirrus
whose role is to extend.

File this away
return to the world skin admits

By sway of sky.

Marginal annotations earlier this morning.

Or sketches of Satie's hand
turns the composition's lightness

To lines of inquiry or texture of the ineffable.

Magenta ring around white hibiscus.

Glint of rufous wing in sunlight.

Toward which view of this parade
will you turn?

If motion is foremost, it's in pattern
or netted aroma

Is where I go when the map runs out.

Bees drown in datura
the falling trellis, Satie's sleep.

The dexterous hand, the darting eye

The rufous ascends
to what Satie circles.

Inhabit or escape
sound remains.

Before Light

for Natalia

In the act of opening illustrations
the words are not mine:
a distant hum . . . faroff buzzings . . .

Plot peeks through a vivid scene
organizes a night's sleep.
The drawings are yours, portion and seed
that I plant, not according to ease.

The pleasing closure, not conceived.
Bring along remembrance, a sip
of coffee, attention, mobile as it strikes.

With small feet on my back. I see you
swimming, foresee you in the surf.
My daughter, you give me lives.

You shine in sleep.
It's your marks in a book, where words
are mine, but thread together,
where I'm breathless, to finish the streak.

Like morning runs before rays strike
sleepless, but with seeing I'm seen.

Your breeze-life keeps me, as I arise
before light, the pane's cold.

Morning sky clear, cerulean.
Your eyes still sleep, lush in their seeing.
You return night's belief
as you would keep me,

I steer, my site, the pages you bring.

quote: Nathaniel Mackey, Whatsaid Serif

WHEELWING

for Dale Kappy

Dusk ghosted embers
tonight Saturn & Jupiter
next to a gibbous moon.

Through dirt trails, thickets
under cottonwood winter,
the sky tangled

twigs & branches.
At high speed, duck head
air dervished, a slipstream

behind my bike.

•

Next to the swollen river
a bump gets through.
You're a Buddha known
as The Sunbather.

If the edges of twigs
lead to the trunk
its annular rings act
still in visible worlds.

Lunar eclipse, ghost sign riverward.
As if echoed under shadow
a luminous haze.

Seep back to the pump up
a hill, legs extend, hands pull
the bike ascends,
front wheel bites

off music sharply
in the turns, brakes
what points persist.

•

A few lines created from the wheel
from the locomotive lunar sky.

The dirt that sticks
hours on a bike

go round in
certain infrared embers

ghosted in curious wind.

OUT TO see

The properties of flame in a fine
tipped pen—in the scaffolding
of ocean words
in constant chant might tear
late sort enter stillness
to state fissures exist, an
honor sown high up, the alphabet
also in clouds stream over
rock to catch the first rays
and reverberate in the skull
a day sculpts, fans forward
on stones, before eyesight
does color exist?
                    I want new
pigments in the music that draws in
moving targets, goals, to
work them over in the flesh side
footstrength of handflocks
waterfalls, torrents, wind tunnels,
geese signs point
flight veer. Kite rides
rain thunder, a saw bites
through black ant trails the
catastrophe, sideways glances
cliff house loops back to
the flesh, makes words form,

dissolve, build only so far,
resist reduction, during rush
hour sweat on the face, anxiety's
visual embrace, numbness or
is it a hum against the skull?
Not to call too early, but
drum ride aerial views along
the shore, speed the sun against
sky watch time lapse into the see
of us all, leaves of excitement
compact with each beat
of the drum concerto again
branches back to a *sotto voce*
size inside the visual frame
an avalanche in the alphabet
as fast as mass in time lapse
past the powersurge
unprotected screams inside, donkey
boat, mule beat, picking through
debris for some insight, or to
make a living at the edge of words
where they cast off into over
around through the partial as
the first rays pervade morning,
measure it against the bare cherry trees
winter half over more what happens
when I've awakened too early

flame plays, we cannot talk if I
can warn you, these chains of
words build paradise, prisons, too,
many times overcome
wave light frequency in
temple sight changes flame
as it heads out to see

in conjunction with the film Baraka *by Ron Fricke*

SHORING THE TIDE

for Natalia

Who, if you splashed in the wave,
would lend you wings?

In imaginal landscapes
you enter silent readings

to provoke white breath, blue & green
dreams. Relentless daughter

I want to sate your hunger.
The cry of absolutes

a rush through the tide.
In surf side hours

I learn how to blend.
Rainwater dripping, nights received.

Soft on the feet, dreamwork
steady, overlaps. Waves delete

completion, the continual conceived.
What roots among the factual

the imaginal unfurls,
infers among its footnotes

in childrift, receipt.
How to tie a knot

behind the back, or ease
some memory granted

surety to untie it
through thwart or skill

to appease a daughter's spleen.
As this shriek in shimmers

ripples light waves
where I keep you

from rushing into surf.
Brief clues allow love

to cup knowledge,
perform in the same play.

It's in glee our eyes meet
sport climb endeavors grace

momentum adds retrieval
lashes bundle's trace.

I try to read you
the book of arrivals

but you launch departures
in consistent mirrors or darts.

Like any other excursion
we perform a passage of surprise

and leave the rest to sneeze.
Blank sky, touring splice

on wide screen projection
or narrowly in an eyelash,

wisp, or scream.
In motion or dread of freeze

you're fearless in face and limb.
So much the ocean or osprey

wing, wave or slight of breath.
When tide rushes toward me

I hold you in the spread.

ISLAND VARIATIONS

for Jon Halper & Yvonne Marquis

1

Work from round stones, pebbles, mercury
in mind.

Line blend salal, scallop shells.

On the edge of the woods, alder
where some fire'd been.

Body a harbor, wreathe, sandslide
as thrown, mixed.

On the outer blue of sound
the shade receives

Blackberries, figs, cherry jam, scones.

Shark Reef samples best of the airspray
inhabits the reed wind muscles.

Gathering bits of wood, not moving an inch.

Refresh what takes over, climbs.

Distant hammering on the breeze.

We pass over the pavement
not to complete what's seen

Toward solace among leaves and early chill.

A partial content shapes, funnels.

Or by deed, rock vein startles
amused identities.

When I scan meridians, enclosures,
cover-horizons.

Canada geese like an unclasped necklace
in the sky.

2

From mercury in pebbles, stone round mind
works motion.

A lone salmon jumps
seals on the islet mid-day heat.

From driftbranch to log
I go back without touching the sand.

Quail run on the side of the road
damsel fly's double wings transparent.

A housedoor slam carries the wind clearly.

In this world, too, part of an edge.

Losing count of the holes in log.

What narrative resides in driftwood bark:

The hawk wheels, sketches island range.

No Overnight Moorage
a crow does not concede.

Swallows dive and dart
fan the air provides.

2:40 pm, moss on hand cut shakes.

Queen Anne's lace, poppies, thistles.

Tide catches the sun mode ripples.

3

Mercury round mind, stones,
works, pebbles

Off blue inch clarity, flight,
jutting rock.

9:30 am, awake four hours, islands drift.

Foot voice meters keep time in chill
stain on the deck.

Rays fathom water shadow
spokes round my head.

How curious the costumes bright voices surround.

Dryness of the feet, wetness the envelope
heat the ferry dissipates.

Occupy this place as color,
scent, texture, residue.

Wake of the ferry boat
more fleet than I expect.

Toward which instant, movement, or place?
As statement, shadow, forest, sound.

A nasty fall, abrasion and bruise on the shin
you'll not forget.

San Juan de Fuca cove
the Olympics covered by fog and clouds.

Fern drip on my face, rocks swim the tide.

Shades of azure, emerald, turquoise.

5:50 pm, I arise in slight inklings
sand between toes.

Hemlocks almost to the end of the island cave.

A rearrangement of pebbles and intestines
selfsame action as the sky.

4

Pebbling mercury works from round stones, mind.

Kelpblends in footprints.

When the Olympics appear, day turns about face.

11:53 am, light barely gets through logged woods
seeks its own release.

A slug chews a dandelion.

Tiderise, rockshout, tentfly fills with wind.

Continuity has a discrete vocabulary
floats kelpbeds.

From this rockseat vantage
a chorus of waves.

Whitecaps proceed by their own equations.

Does sight or sound arrange these lines?

3:47 pm, waiting for water to boil.

When I look back, the dandelion's gone.

Stumps in these woods a reminder of power overhead.

3 am, no starblaze history of fog.

A lone glacier, the variable tide, time divides.

Hair curls moist air currents.

The sand in a square foot
multiplies an endless niche.

Your shin, three days later, begins to mend.

At the construction site eelgrass, a cedar branch
our vertical climb out of the cove.

The water hot, coffee brewed
steam meets the well-tuned gaze.

IMPROVISATION BEGINNING WITH LINES BY ROSMARIE WALDROP

                              I traced the law
                of suffiicient reason
                              down
                    your spine
              played calligraphy
                        that spells viscera
        what food
                              I remember
            that slumber
                    comes undone
          a banquet spread
                                      how
            the tongue's fugue
                doubles back
            pitches
              a sly jest
                    the curved neuron's
                delicious response
        a grace I paid
                  the patterns change
          charge vertebrae   in-
            scribe
                        a novel lesson
              screen   the angles
                    distances affect ascent
                    measure slant meridians

                      quote: Reproduction of Profiles

46

Broken Light

Part dislocation, part re-rooting
distinction matched and mounting
sieve through so many books and letters

try to pack sort time rumors
we only have so much
to mail ourselves an article
or sign to put on our plates
more toward evening

as night sheathes sleep
trouble in back strain combo
north of the body's equator
sown spine and trope of goodness
in a further ladder leading down.

Part liberation, part stockade
reclothe phantom strains
retell fleeting chambers
where room opens outward

to courier documents between abodes
with our own soothsaying
washer drier, to spy on

house dimensions, stairs, chimney
sport ivy feeling rough seat
heave onto higher shelves.

Backyard asters,
sun filters zinnias, marigolds
rays through grapeleaves
in the diurnal turning alone

in place to catch in throat
deep inhale blur
cherry trees blink
eyes rest on Mexican sage.

Slow exhale, further
along my legs,
I stretch my head
clear sight ivy to pull

and see lawn that needs
digging out climb
strip off of pines
to preserve the pulse.

As a boy I cut the cancerous growth
ivy can be, bagged not composted.

Books and papers
to navigate, reread, sort,
order as wind riffles
flight takes shape.

Not know but make present.

Set out the terms
engage the move, one
foot, then another,
in discrete bits, continues

a reel of action, subtle domains
while back legs hands heave
sofa, tables, cabinets, sink.

Find the threads, weave,
run through visuals,
see motion leaves stillness
in its blend juniper pine.

•

Willow morning air,
sit on cold cushions,
to seat flow through
cold bare feet.

Part risk, part safety
rufous wings in constant motion
dawn sky shatters clouds.

Now sipping nectar, night
not entirely gone.
Broken light waves over Sandias.

What keeps attention in front
maintains in the roots' reception.
See what can be shed.
Like shaking drops of water off
instead of reverberating rage.

In grief music twists intestines
inverted arteries, broken organs
letters of transit, the chance to report

over and against the human interest
and maelstrom's disease.
Slice a ripe tomato
juice plate light salt.

Pick buds on basil
feel toe ankle stretch through dis-
comfort, notice burn blister index
finger formed overnight.

If I can lengthen the area of stretch
back strain soreness loosens the cords
where hands connect
I sit next to a willow,
in search of radicles' keep.

•

Part construction, part enactment
map with all its roads gone blank.
Still what's scattered on the floor.

Locate letters I want.

Down a dark hallway, stairs.
Underfeet purring sounds
through moving frames.

Overhead feet jump sort
through the soothe
a race is on.

What echoes to the side?

Turkish rug inside of door.
The white red black

patterns almost Pueblo.
Satie gives strength in grief.

Cry not what's denied
in perspiration, seed & nerve.
Feet thump & bless
in situ, tomatoes ripening still

on vine directs light
to tap autumnal equinox
poised in the turning pain.

Sight set on the unborn
what soil radicles would nourish.
Rise 4:50 am, guided by lamps
outside pupils' wide angle

every chance to increase nightsight.
Push on lamps, lengthen measure
pupils contract in glare
initial contact, each new day awaits.

What ceiling I'd bring
to any given register, switch
places, define them anew
with each reading, lives

take place, form possibility
in a rhythm that is one
of Satie's "Crooked Dances."

How to stream upstairs
percuss the piano keys.
Fire states the first spark,
circles the stones a ring makes.

One flashes under the stump.
One springs the brightened table.
One catapults mud.

Of time made night
arrangements, shade.
Morning rise quiet, Satie's parade.

•

Part parallel, part discrete
where soil meets mixture
hands me color as currency
blue in energy's charge, brown
sound of feet run above me.

Morning chill, window flung
open where oxygen

plants action, patterns
design stones thrown
open in a circle, coal stump.

Embered flakes of ash, then,
apposite rainstick shakes
contrasts darksky's invention.

Where redemption's available
the given is gained
in the hand's commission
a rhythmic tranced
sea change, title flame.

•

Part depth, part screen
to flee analogy

while continuing the seem.
No vague document
but an opening oblique.

Remaining in sound is hearing
textures, pain, ruminations' cue.
Basil buds flowered
require more stamina, rest.

Condensation on window
before first light hits.
Easy answer in visual deeds.

Cat crouched, refrigerator's
motor, feels heat.
Palms together provide energy
to complete a cycle.

Only what flies to see and hear.
The way hands wrap toes
leg extended to route
electric contact, stadium change.

Reside among trees.
Seed in a crooked dance.
Mulberry, willow, pine.

Circumscribe the wall's outward way.
What sparksigns outside analogy.
The body swings in time's texture
flux & fire, basis & deed.

DUELS & DIVERGENCES

The poets face, move
in the verbal ghetto.

They construct houses so close
to the heat. I tried to stave
off the hurricane.

My bills soar, a critical surplus
of acumen. *For Coolidge*
language is no philosopher's
stone. Ashbery's unbearable
swiftness alights in a corner
of our room.

Our language
inscribes a body in its absence
there is one. I slip up

against reaches, never
disinclined. I would hover
words just over
the outstretched hand.

Word plenty scraped
from the palate. Green

flight moons dare
transpire in saturating
discourse. Purple scales
from the lake.

Draft a number off to war.
When a rose is cut it bleeds
not. Things can suggest
where an absence collapses.

If I salute the questioning,
I read lines of things,
the witness erodes. Move into
the danger zone. The horse
shallows my gallop. Ornette
shifts melodic chordings
in irreducible theme.

I imagine the plays. Springs
are spring-colored. Staff
technique cast bites
into an orange, but
don't take that grant
for *Origin*, Cid.

If the seam is themeless
art folds in on itself.

Organize the words
and watch them revolt.
The sway palms under an intent
sky. Time for immolations
of grammar. Quickly
hardly costly squarely.

Allow hunger to seep in.
Windly move the staunch
thistle. A garden drouths.
Avocado pit slips through
the fingers. Plant damage
in factories' smoke rings.

In assemblage roughed wrinkles
the materials avail themselves.
Shore the walkways down
the melodic line. I descry
a wellness, a bucket.

Place stamp here. String the
fingers, and stand the collection.
No wonder the book upsets
audiences. A television has
never been more than in-
accurate at the outset.

When too much clarity snaps
the pencil in two. How
does it taste? How near
the thinning synapse?

Go back to early morning
stacking books on shelves.
Ideas for letters. Charcoal
drawings with ink outlines.

A thin division between
challenge and wall.
. . . and if I keep skipping
from one story to another
it's because I keep circling
around that story and escaping,
as if it were the first day
of my escape.
On the island

blank books spread out
in all directions. The
choice is revolving and
I can't always.

By the scale of a body
is its seductive potential.

Collected verse separates
by the line. A temblor of
recognition. The book laughs
and forgets the circle of
aggregate dancers. Critics

band claps to the progeny. In
divagations lead the crooked
lines, conspiracies, the scent.
And that boy stirring deranged
ashes in the Commune.
Desert lightning traces my hand.

Reading is going toward
something that is about
to be, and no one yet knows
what it will be. The physicist
descends into the innards
of atoms. The boy becomes

monstrous in his Illuminations.
Between sentences read
clefts in memory. Not just
the supple sleight of hand.
The sweat of fast elaborations.

quotes: Italo Calvino, if on a winter's night a traveler
& Barret Watten, Total Syntax

WITNESS SLIDES

1

Before the rain dipped quiver
shoots an arrow of warped tension,
the witness slides, garbled
by a wad of cash.

Distinctions explode the savings,
loaned to a drifting state.

Squeeze the tentacles, lie
in wait, hunted from
multiple wings, he glances
over the pages of the *Wall Street
Journal*, the subway, smoke rises
up the stairs.
                        The point of public spaces
dissolves. She sets the coffee
down. Drift time percussive
train of commuter swings,
she puffs the cigaret.

2

Before the dipped quiver rains
a pox attacks the immune system.
He sets the *Journal* aside,
throws up his feet too driftly.

In a play dreamed currency,
he exchanges the firm's bullion
for wet thorns and bars.

He sticks to what he does best.
A wing-tipped cipher on spread sheet
rockets to the tune of sentimental gas jets.

She clicks her pumps,
cigaret glows in the puffing room.
In transit the composite portrait
rearranges the line.

She leaves the train

                    places an aura.

3

Before quiver rain dips
the train moves into a square
of hard light. Iridescent in his dream
of tank cadillac shower,
he maps a stunned window

where topography is melody
past his threshold.

Who drank the juice first
when she confiscated the current
on his ambidextrous route?

Utility bills bank the train track.
Faulty carburetor siphons
a rich mixture. She moves in

an utterance of disjunction,
the master cylinder upset.

He would clutch himself, break.

ALL MATTER IS ENCOUNTER

for Stephen Ellis

1

Short clue pertains to amount of memory.
As lightness. All my time has been
going elsewhere. Toward which lives
are out there. That life or more.
Which river at my feet?

When authority is not a function
of social situation. It's a neon dog
across the gaze. In which slides
the right moment. If I'd formally
ring the bone, a precision startles.

Don't send me the warped discourse.
What goes for public dialogue corrodes
thought. Anger and flexibility, the tenuous
force field charges the gray sky.
Winter's half over and snow only once.

Lone crow wheels high, pecan shells
on the street. The buzz voice blurs
what's common, perverse. Not that I wanted
to draw attention to it. To cultivate an ear,
to the table we must bring.

All matter is encounter . . . Portion
of music, not aversion. If history marks
a spot, my narrative's never complete.
To find circles around the room.
A sight belongs the walk in town.

Try us again in Y2K, but no improvisations
next time. Speed and power doubles
every eighteen months. Can you find the dot
in the ink jet? The outlines of mountains.
I'd assume a silhouette in green.

Pavement gives ground. Mortality
or aberration, the hum remains.
Toward gear motion, a pain or splice
of dream. How I'm preparing
for the heat, driven millennium.

Entering the end of beginning.
Credit's a slippery thing. Gamble
against the wire. Fight operations
that crowd the mind out. How many
halogen lights are in this room?

Combine height bleeding
align scope ceiling. Off dawn
runs, the timing. I'll concede
moisture suspends light. Compose
with camera in mind.

Through the French door, the front
of a pick-up. Gray sky persists.
What equals precision in observation?
In action, thought breeds its own
species. Polyrhythms move the body.

Extra directions. Brevity in music leads
to comedy. Short end of the bench
remains without motion or certainty.
Plausibility in intersections, former
adhesions obtain. Ideal audience vs.

real audience. Try to imagine where
I dropped my right glove. Localize
the point, its time and rhythm. If passage
could explain the organism's disposition.
I awake with my skull in another's hands.

Taken in by root or bough. Annoyed at
the replaceable loss. Whatever else
attention can be extended. Voice blend
distinction, the wire conducts composition.
Awaken too early Saturday morning.

Window twists conditioning
the sky still gray. So we sit on
the deck and wait for it to turn.
Sooner than expected
you examine the dried stem

of a grapevine. As though to
pull apart, you organize textures.
Winter heat alive, 1:58 pm.
What stirs the book brings you back
to the page. Then to see

the wrappers in others' hands.
The precise shape of ocher
you imagine sliced into an arroyo, sky.
What makes the notebook available
is a daughter playing with dried grapes.

Return to the bicycle ride 11 am.
Cholla, chamisa line the trail.
The quality of motion stretches out
as if to bring distance much closer.
At which cadence, the shift occurs.

Into a lower gear, the rocks climb at you.
Ply dirt, torque leg enforcement.
I take the grapes away.   Not before
you've eaten one or two. Winter allows
heat arrests ordinary surprise.

Calm leaves it a verb, though
nominal at best. We pat on the slats
of the chair just to see the window shake.
You engage textures of the wood,
weigh sunlight, travel.

What's brought to the mix alters the meal.
Shine battle moves, exactly within what's dull.
The range of our pedaling up the wash
to refresh bikework I'd receive.
But I pour out verbs even in pale winter light.

2

What portion is sky itself? If I want the rose to turn air flame,
pruning's necessary. Size of the story's contingent on texture of the plan.
Alter slightly the letters you receive and the poem's fleshed out.

Improvisation in attention to the sound or color that ignites.
Forest blue night leaves, the foliage of cannas. As if to slide
through Cezanne. No accomplices better equipped. The books
concede: a portion of art sticks to the wall.

Return them to Gene. If only slightly still, diverse the preserve.
Provocation or perversity, letters unfold in the instant.
Although brief, the work extends in digestion. Algorithm
for laying bare. The oblique spreads out its axes.
Halogen lamp hums until sleep takes me one row, then another.

I turn the lamp brighter, search night's labor to supplant rest.
A fresh orange away, light commitment. Coarse indigo
eye on the rain we're lacking. Wool gloves thin
where the bike handles rub. F(r)iction in the midst
of cinders, a glass of stream water.

Encounter does matter, all eating aside. Then slipped out of my skin
to begin the voyage. Name a color of spectral grace,
sketch a sunflower the right shade

or place the scent of an aurora that always eludes.
I ladle out clouds with soup. I want something more than aural background,
music in a pinch. Still the chair has to conform to physiology.

Marks on the paper can stand for musical tone in time.
All the background sound washes over focused listening.
Soft architecture stretches over the scent of ecstasy.
The public hallucinates daily and calls it news.

Pursue those areas of awareness in the face that turns it
into a body. Like a gland irritated by overstimulation,
you throw off endorphins. The unconscious in a flea market.

A cup covered with fur, a clothes iron with tacks glued on.
Snapshots of the impossible: bureaucrats
commuting to work from heaven, the train out of the fireplace.

Plus votes, lunatics get you elected. Quality of shadows lengthen,
5:02 pm, February 11. Coldness cleans the nasal hairs,
silhouettes lost to surprise. If it were just a matter to encounter.

When the obvious is not opaque,
sit next to the window, without seeing the breeze.
Not that I don't take it seriously
exactly, but matter moves all the time. That narrows it down
to every poem that's ever been written. I come to the café
to escape distraction. Background hum becomes familiar

as conversation with an edge. When I try to lengthen
my bridge, the words themselves condense. To write
is to consult with your faculties and expand the enclosures.

Toward a tunnel, the home inside the room. As Mary often reminds me,
to alter the syntax is to arrest new color, sound. He pokes
his head in the door to see if anyone familiar is here.
Shoes conduct electricity, but do all encounters have matter?

Organize the stanzas, and watch the method revolt.
As the door swings open, a draught of freezing air.
Arouse sight acute, spare as tea, the cadence is in feeling.
Brush it so that every stroke counts. In Satie
there is no wasted note. In any art, hand times the measure.

What proportions are in session? I like blue and yellow rhythms.
The line of people coming in the door lengthens. Benjamin's
essay on the *flâneur*. Say if the name recalls something in the future.

Inquiry can press into new countries.
How the present represents itself, a poet away. Not entirely
a function of audience. When my feet get cold, it's time
to start a fire. Let's say it's a matter of fit.

Satie moves toward perpetual gesture. He circles the café again,
anxious to find conversation. The aroma of brownies
just before bedtime. I'd pay attention to breath, so I don't hold it
in composition, turn out, ceiling. He persists in great phrasing.

Sleep overcomes the last thought. Shape line briefly so
syllables earn their sound. For brevity a good night's rest.
Think back to where you were when you took the glasses off.
Not a tight horn conclusion, the wave that comes to inhabit the home.

In every small crack, the journey's not exact,
made possible by a son who chips away on stone.
Rehearsals for the archaic in a four year-old.
Resources add to magnetism.

Bacteria mutate to feed on us. The body must seize,
be seized. Early afternoon, you bounce in a seat.
When exactly did the sublime bite the dust? If all else fails,
functional habit serves.

The car in front of us blares bass stereo, distorts our sound.
The rivulet brings the distant close, joins far off intimacies,
states what water only can bestow.

3

When I jump particles in the sky
true solvent motion in anatomy of sense.

It's not really just a place to eat
but a nexus to exchange dialogue.

For portion scene probability, consult a circular almanac.
Gustaf Sobin follows syllable length, sound in tile or dream,

the made place, folded again
whether Taos or Provence, landscape plays.

Between the insight and event, "exquisite convolutions."
A flower chair whose bell admits soft announcements.

Ride a bike jump claims of light in motion.
What part of encounter matters?

The sky potions light anchors.
Sheila Murphy's lines work continually

at school or office, desert or relief.
In cadence brightening, split open riddles

she leads currency into the shape of surprise.
I have to cycle home again to the sweep in felicity.

I note what visuals are in the language
and open time toward late afternoon.

How sunlight strikes the plain at different angles of the season.
Separated from the city by plate glass windows

a vantage point permits an eye more matter.
I wake with sight of violet blue transition, 5:09 am,

so that there is a hall therein . . .
Years now to maintain reach in body, extend tendons.

The car wreck I avoid, almost cause, plagues judgment
sound island, deepsea. I can see what you're saying

but the relations *are* causal, even disconnect hinges.
Live wires in Sheila's haibun.

Within house kindness, sly warmth, intimacies speculate, renew.
5:49 pm, sundown spreads out, the sky not bare;

dusk sight leans, high clouds wheel.
The acrid scent of roasting coffee burns the air.

Something of the sound texture of the room.
What couples itself together, hears apart.

The two eat in silence. In the window
freesight waits, charmed and hovering.

Little feet against my back. Awake just
after midnight, the parade in dada skirts.

They shovel their food down
avert eyes from each other.

The windows open, 8:15 pm, February 27.
The man suddenly animates the air around his wife.

He stumbles an airjet behind him
swirled subatomic cynicism.

To awake just after midnight, you
sit up beside me, whimpering.

Not the sum total of lines
those that extend the inexpressible.

"There and not there." On the page
and what surrounds, challenges.

Do I want to write or go for a ride?
Sight past limits, treaties with the unseen.

To be inside defaults this day.
Distinction carries through Sobin's work

makes ordinary electric scoop mandala
painting talus or cerulean, Cezanne,

if he lived here now. Pigments in the poem
verbs in the paint. Words, in other worlds,

taste hunger, violet in continual change.

4

Claim the sky's weight unseen.
For strophe or motion,
encounter times form, the dense matters in seeing.

The poem of hall voice confusion passing,
in the wave, mass art collusion.
What circles around the room size buzz, not tornado.
This range falls, a gathering, chief fandango,

in all arts of learning, articulation.
In composition of the crystalline, Clark Coolidge
turns quartz eye solutions, facets improv's lot,
assumes syncopation.

Sound that thinks, thought that resounds.
The hum of the room improves me.
The last bit of juice tastes best.

After a few hours, the sound of Coolidge remains.
"This staying put" which travels out
toward sight, refrains. How sound affects
the resource, soon enough,

where the right rhythm sorts it out.
I hope your neck isn't stiff when you wake.

Milky twilight, moisture needed.
Dada portraits, shaggy in a room

without alphabet, exactly. When I think I've found
the nexus of the room, it alters, my thought
partial, responsible. Compatible demonstrations
to be desired. It's not where to travel,

but what to bring to the location. As under the feet
surrounding the house, the cold air.
To quiet or incite, no question but commission.
Thoreau, if he lived in Petaluma.

This place where morning is permanent
fly lust early, not deferred.
You wake up in good cheer, neck supple.

Give me a dirty car to avoid, and I'll find a blank page.
The crystal almost invisible in taking on and in
the tones of everything else in the room . . .
picks up the energy, values the very hum,

violet in range. What you show up with
in elation or reprieve. All branches of
the pine shake the wind. How you punctuate
commas, matters. The (con)science

of perception will provide. At what point
do you line it in flame? This window's my
crystal, portrait view, but it's what anyone

brings to the window that matters.
How you move the frame depends on
the referent, context not rent-free.
Refers to energy at any time available,

imaginative. Where I have to walk
everyday, a chaos fights agenda.
Again next to my window, the rush of the hall

into one voice, commercial traffic.
Release hormones, the size of work toward learning
where to invest the energies.
Snow reflects the light wet hiding.
Feet moist touring, I walk out of the room.

Infinity and the limit exist side by side.
What energy locates places the room.
Demolitions permit remodeling to proceed.

Hunger as value propels the body through time.
The room, then, exacts this crystal hum
as the lattices open. In what way do the unseen
places intercede? Or plant sound last

photography in terms of breadth, longitude.
Fractions, portions of what we receive, see:
sleep colors it all in. Just the right trace
of humor; channels for outrage,
an eye on one's own actions.

When each note matters, encounter
delivers on its own terms. Satie sends you in a round
accompanied by ripe gestures whose brevities

pass in and out of intensity. To rush or to rest,
the toll still waits. Rhythm drives tempo
in relation to the seeds.

quotes: Clark Coolidge, The Crystal Text
& Robert Duncan, The Opening of the Field

Brooklyn & Back

Clouds framed in the atrium
drift fine recombinations.
Now the slivers of
voices from David's shelves
unbind books born rattling.

A glad act proclaims the verbal
handspring. Not an entertaining
film, the frames untamed
in this reel. *The most
photographed bridge in the world.*
"I too am not a bit tamed . . ."
The cable spider filaments to web
suspension tossed supreme.
Please let me ride the breakers.
Or the throngs crossing
right now that touch a century
later, that Brooklyn burst sameness.
The stingy spring in my face
blasts the chilled veins' retreat.

•

Reach back for everything left.
The pigments turn a fractal stream.
A table that overwhelms the palate.

Scan back the jagged teeth of Manhattan
from Mailer's porch. Forsythia sends
the fragile release. Potted tulips
between iron railings.
Foot of the bridge, building plaque
an abolitionist fired from *The Brooklyn Eagle.*
I might be looking at you.
"And goodbye to you too, old *Rights of Man!*"

Stake out the proper mutiny.
Not published till 33 years after
Melville's last sentence.

No smoking in this café.
No rays on the bridge horizon
the promenade's last insistence.
The sky's rifle gray. Slip time's
irrevocable march, a mute
lapse of sequence.

•

I play swirls of cream and coffee.
In my cup, worlds surprise.
You might be looking at me.
Whitman's line a century later
declines an interview.

A jet roar samizdat distracts
the atrium's light. *Community*
tunnels under the skin, subverts
the puppet master. Starting out
from the lion steps, drizzle fogs
eyeglasses. A taxi uptown.
Who plunges into Melville's ambiguities?
Our stride rattles the century's past.
A broken umbrella, the worn woman cries.
The sailor stutters an odd abyss:
bright demons burn the soles of shoes.

John Tritica is co-founder, with Mary Rising Higgins, of L)Edge, a poetry circle twenty-years-old this year. He is translator of Swedish poet Niklas Törnlund's *All Things Measure Time* (The Landlocked Press, 1992). Author of the collection *How Rain Records Its Alphabet* (La Alameda Press, 1998), his poetry, translations and critical work have appeared in a wide range of publications. He teaches gifted students at Wilson Middle School in Albuquerque, while raising a garden with his family.

Chax Press programs and publications are supported by donations
from individuals and foundations, as well as from the Tucson Pima
Arts Council and the Arizona Commission on the Arts, with funding
from the State of Arizona and the National Endowment for the Arts.

Arizona
Commission
on the Arts

NATIONAL
ENDOWMENT
FOR THE ARTS

TUCSON PIMA
ARTS
COUNCIL

Some Recent and Forthcoming Books from Chax Press

Fiction

Hilton Obenzinger, *Busy Dying*
Kass Fleisher, *Accidental Species*

Poetry

Jeanne Heuving, *Transducer*
Elizabeth Treadwell, *Wardolly*
Karen Mac Cormack, *Implexures II*
Steve McCaffery, *Slightly Left of Thinking*
Michael Cross, *In Felt Treeling*
Bruce Andrews, *Swoon Noir*
Tim Peterson, *Since I Moved In*
Paul Naylor, *Arranging Nature*
Sarah Riggs, *Waterwork*
Glen Mott, *Analects on a Chinese Screen*
Charles Borkhuis, *Afterimage*
Beth Joselow, *Begin At Once*
Linh Dinh, *Jam Alerts*
Linda Russo, *Mirth*
Joe Amato, *Under Virga*

Artist's Book Editions / Book Arts Works

Kathleen Fraser and Nancy Tokar Miller, *Witness*

More books, and more information about Chax Press, appear on our web site: http://chax.org.